Getting started
Max science Enquiry Box 3

CB082299
9781380019936

Welcome to Max Science Enquiry Box 3: hands-on science out of the box! These hands-on activities, guided discussions and diverse experiments allow for student-driven lessons across Chemistry, Biology and Physics while building key Scientific Enquiry skills. Remember to access your online resources, including step-by-step Teacher's Notes, by activating the codes on the sticker inside your box at **www.macmillaneducationeverywhere.com**. For customer service, please visit **help.macmillan.com**.

The author and publishers would like to thank the following for permission to reproduce their images:

Biology cards: Getty Images pp16 (elephant), 22 (canteen), 30 (apple), 30 (peach), 30 (pear), Getty Images/eli_asenova p30 (orange), Getty Images/EyeWire p40 (goldfish), Getty Images/Hero Images/Hero Images p23 (l), Getty Images/iStockphoto/PeopleImages p16 (girl), Getty Images/iStockphoto/Thinkstock p40 (cat), Getty Images/iStockphoto/Thinkstock/Andrey Armyagov p20 (meal), Getty Images/iStockphoto/Thinkstock Images/Sascha Burkard p40 (frog), Getty Images/iStockphoto/Thinkstock Images/Carmelka p30 (banana), Getty Images/iStockphoto/Thinkstock Images/et_engineer p40 (fly), Getty Images/iStockphoto/Thinkstock/Igor Shirobokov p16 (tv), Getty Images/iStockphoto/Thinkstock Images/sommail p40 (locust), Getty Images/iStockphoto/Thinkstock Images/Rafal Szostek p40 (small fish), Getty Images/iStockphoto/Thinkstock Images/Camilo Torres p14 (rat), Getty Images/iStockphoto/Thinkstock/Ameng Wu p40 (snake), Getty Images/Kryssia Campos p16 (hummingbird), Getty Images/PhotoDisc pp13 (plant), 14 (chick), 14 (elephants), 16 (stones), 14 (cheetah), 16 (glass of water), 23 (m), 33 (bread), 35, 40 (butterfly), 40 (lizard), Getty Images/Thinkstock/John Foxx p40 (bull); **Image Source** p16 (cactus), ImageSource p36; **Macmillan Publishers Ltd**/Paul Bricknell p16 (vase). **Biology worksheets: ComStock Images** p20 (g), **Digital Vision** p28 (bear), **Getty Images** pp21 (apple), 21 (peach), 21 (pear), 28 (tiger), 28 (iguana), Getty Images/Dirk Ercken Photography p28 (frog), Getty Images/Dorling Kindersley/Thinkstock Images/Dave King p20 (b), Getty Images/eli_asenova p21 (orange), Getty Images/John Gollop p20 (c), Getty Images/iStockphoto/scanrail p20 (e), Getty Images/iStockphoto/Thinkstock Images/Carmelka p21 (banana), Getty Images/iStockphoto/Thinkstock/Evgeny Terentev p20 (a); **John Foxx Images** pp28 (l, ml); **Macmillan Publishers Ltd**/Stuart Cox p20 (d), Macmillan Publishers Ltd/Macmillan Australia p25 (b), Macmillan Publishers Ltd/Macmillan Mexico/Tony Sanchez p28 (ladybug); **PhotoDisc**/Getty Images p28 (beetle), PhotoDisc p28 (bumblebee), PhotoDisc/Getty Images p28 (snake).

Chemistry cards: Brand X p10 (socks); **Corbis**/Royalty Free p3 (metal toy car); **Getty Images** p3 (scissors), Getty Images/Dorling Kindersley RF/Thinkstock/Howard Shooter p10 (baseball cap), Getty Images/EyeWire p3 (wooden blocks), Getty Images/Hemera/Thinkstock Images/Kathleen Melis p3 (plastic spoon), Getty Images/Hemera/Thinkstock/Dmitriy Tereschenko p10 (coat), Getty Images/iStockphoto/gofotograf p10 (shirt), Getty Images/iStockphoto/Thinkstock p10, Getty Images/iStockphoto/Thinkstock Images/Jitalia17 p10 (trousers), Getty Images/iStockphoto/Thinkstock/Elena Milevska p10 (t-shirt), Getty Images/iStockphoto/Thinkstock Images/olm26250 p5 (magnet), Getty Images/PhotoDisc p3 (pencils), Getty Images/Paul Wiese/EyeEm p9; **Image Source** p3 (paper clip); **Macmillan Publishers Ltd**/Paul Bricknell p6, Macmillan Publishers Ltd/Haddon Davies p3 (teddy bear), Macmillan Publishers Ltd/Macmillan Australia p3 (metal spoon); **Shutterstock**/Natan86 p10 (red sweater); **Stockbyte Royalty Free Photos** p3 (plastic toy car, plastic cup).

Physics cards: BananaStock p7; **Getty Images**/Photodisc/Digital Vision, Getty Images/Thinkstock Images/Fuse p3.

Scientific enquiry

Scientific Enquiry

Stage 3

Scientific Enquiry skills		Biology cards	Chemistry cards	Physics cards
Ideas and evidence	Collect evidence by making observations when trying to answer a science question. (3Ep1)	2, 4, 6, 9, 13, 20, 25, 35	1, 6	4, 10
Plan investigative work	Suggest ideas, make predictions and communicate these. (3Ep2)	4, 5, 6, 8, 9	5, 6, 8, 9	10
	With help, think about collecting evidence and planning fair tests. (3Ep3)	5, 6, 7, 13, 25	6, 9	10
Obtain and present evidence	Observe and compare objects, living things and events. (3Eo1)	2, 3, 4, 7, 14, 16, 28, 31	3, 10	1, 3, 5, 7
	Measure using simple equipment and record observations in a variety of ways. (3Eo2)	2, 3, 4, 5, 6, 7, 8, 9, 32	8, 9	2, 3, 10
	Present results in drawings, bar charts and tables. (3Eo3)	2, 4, 5, 6, 7, 9, 24, 30, 38	1, 8	7, 8
Consider evidence and approach	Draw conclusions from results and begin to use scientific knowledge to suggest explanations. (3Eo4)	3, 4, 5, 6, 7, 8, 9, 25, 38	8, 9	8, 10
	Make generalisations and begin to identify simple patterns in results. (3Eo5)	2, 4, 10, 13, 18, 27, 29, 40	5	3, 10

Biology

Plants

1: Remember plant parts

Objectives

Know that plants have roots, leaves, stems and flowers.

Use the words in the box to help you to label the plant.

Key words stem flower roots leaf

2: Looking at leaves

Objectives

Know that plants have roots, leaves, stems and flowers.

Stay safe!

Tell your teacher if you have any allergies linked to plants.
Check with your teacher before you pick any leaves.

1. Collect five leaves from different plants.
   a. Draw your leaves. **b.** Compare the leaves. **c.** How are they the same? **d.** How are they different?
2. Measure the size of the leaves using graph paper as shown below. Your results will be in square centimetres (cm^2).

1 square = $1cm^2$

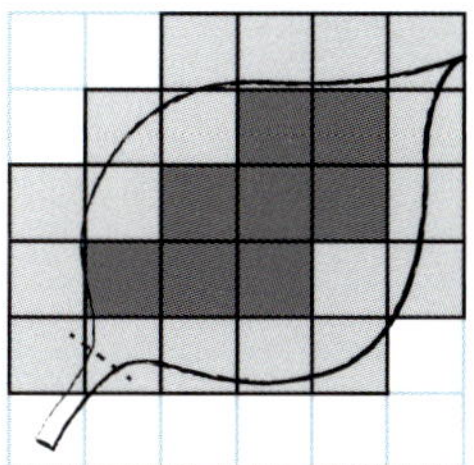

1 square = $1cm^2$

3. Record your observations and measurements in a table.

Talk about Why are leaves important to plants?

Plants

3: What do stems do?

Objectives

Know that plants have roots, leaves, stems and flowers.

You will need some card, scissors, dry spaghetti and sticky tape.

1. Cut out six leaf shapes from your card.
   - **a.** Fix two of your leaves onto a model stem made from one strand of spaghetti.
   - **b.** Shake the stem and blow the leaves.
   - **c.** Record what happens.
2. Fix two leaves to a thicker stem by taping five strands of spaghetti together.
   - **a.** Shake this stem and blow the leaves.
   - **b.** Record what happens.
3. Look at the last two leaves on the table.
   - **a.** Blow on them.
   - **b.** Record what happens.

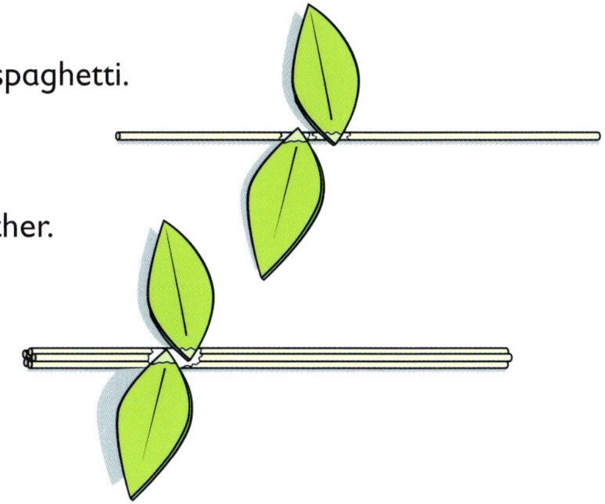

4. Use your investigation results to decide which of the following sentences is **true**. There may be more than one.
   - Plants do not need stems. Leaves do not need to be in sunlight.
   - Stems are important as they hold leaves and flowers in place.
   - Stems hold leaves up high so they catch more sun.
   - Stems are needed to link the roots to the leaves and flowers.
   - It doesn't matter if stems break.

Plants

4: Important roots

Objectives

Know that plants have roots, leaves, stems and flowers.

- Look at the picture.
- Identify the roots.
- Why do the roots have to be so large for this tree?

Investigating roots

Your teacher will take you to a place where you can pull up three different weeds.

1. Draw the weeds.
2. Predict how big the roots will be for each plant.
3. Pull up the weeds.
4. How easy was it to pull the plants up?
5. Wash the leaves.
6. Measure the length of the roots for each plant.
7. Record your observations and measurements in a table.
8. Were your predictions correct?
9. Use your root investigation to help you to write down one important function of roots.

Stay safe!

Tell your teacher if you have any allergies linked to plants.

5: Do plants need light?

Objectives

Explain observations that plants need water and light to grow.

1. One of these plants has been kept in the dark.

   a. Is it plant A or plant B?

   b. What evidence did you use to help you to decide?

2. Plan an investigation to show that plants need light to grow healthily.

   a. Write down your plan.

   b. Include a prediction and a method.

   c. Carry out your investigation and record your findings.

   d. Write a conclusion.

3. Create a presentation of your findings. You could talk to the class or make a large poster.

Plants

6: Helping a dying plant

Objectives

Explain observations that plants need water and light to grow.

A gardener thought that the plant in the picture was dying because it was in the dark.

But after he put the plant in the sunlight for a few days, it continued to die. The gardener then thought the plant might need other things as well as light.

Your teacher will give you a plant that isn't healthy.

- Investigate how to revive a dying plant.
- What factors will help?
- How can you revive the plant?
- Try out your ideas and see if they work.

7: Water and roots

Objectives

Know that water is taken in through the roots and transported through the stem.

Stay safe!

Tell your teacher if you have any allergies linked to plants.
Wash your hands after handling plants and soil.

Your teacher will give you a small potted plant.

1. Carefully remove it from the soil and rinse the roots in running water.
2. Place your plant in a transparent container of water.
3. Cover the container using cling film or clear plastic. This will stop water being lost.
4. Measure the height of the water level and mark it with a marker pen. This is your initial or first reading.
5. Measure and mark the water level at the same time each day for a week.
6. Record your readings in a table and use them to plot a graph.
7. What conclusions can you draw from your findings about the functions of the root system?
8. Create a laboratory report or wiki describing your investigation and your conclusions.

8: Moving water

Objectives

Know that water is taken in through the roots and transported through the stem.

You will work with a small group.
Your teacher will give you a plant.

1. Stand the plant in a container of water.
2. Add food colouring to the water and leave the plant to stand.
3. Predict what you think will happen.
4. Observe your plant every 10 minutes for 40 minutes.
5. Record your findings. This can be by taking measurements, drawing your plant or taking digital photographs.
6. What do your findings tell you about the functions of the stem?
7. Was your prediction correct?

Talk about

Share your ideas with the class as part of a class discussion.

Plants

9: Investigating watering

Objectives

Know that water is taken in through the roots and transported through the stem.

Your teacher will give you some seedlings.

1. Plan an investigation to find out the correct volume of water to give seedlings.
2. Make a list of the equipment you will use.
3. Make a prediction.
4. Carry out your plan safely and record your findings.
5. Was your prediction correct?
6. Present your findings as an information leaflet for gardeners.

10: Working together

Objectives

Know that plants need healthy roots, leaves and stems to grow well.

The person in the picture is taking all of the leaves from this plant! Predict what will happen to the plant.

You are going to investigate how the parts of a plant are all needed for healthy growth. Decide which part of the plant you are going to investigate. This could be leaves, stems or roots. You will be given two identical plants.

1. Remove the part of the plant you are investigating from one of the plants.

Stay safe!

Be careful when cutting your plant.

2. Replant both plants into separate pots and leave them in a sunny place.
3. Water the plants exactly the same for one week.
4. Compare the plants after a week.
5. What conclusions can you draw?
6. Compare your results with people who have investigated other plant parts.

Talk about

What do the investigations tell you about how all of the different parts of a plant are needed for healthy growth?

11: Comparing plants

Objectives

Know that plants need healthy roots, leaves and stems to grow well.

The table below shows some of the causes of plant damage.

Plant damage	Possible cause
Wilting – leaves are sagging	Not enough water
Leaves falling off	Too much water – overwatering
Yellowing of leaves	Poor quality of soil or compost
Very slow growth	Pot too small for the roots

1. Look at the pictures.
2. Identify the most likely cause of the damage in each case.
3. Suggest one solution to each problem.

A

B

C

Plants

12: Identifying plant parts

Objectives

Know that plants need healthy roots, leaves and stems to grow well.

- Study the two plants shown.
- Draw a picture of each plant.
- Label the plant parts by identifying the roots, stems and leaves.

13: Investigating temperature and plant growth

Objectives

Know that plant growth is affected by temperature.

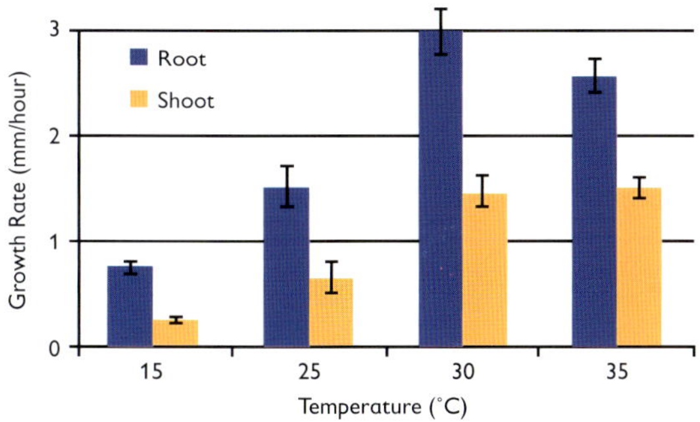

Plants do not grow healthily if it is too hot or too cold.

The graph shows the effect of temperature on the growth of corn plants. It shows how many millimetres per hour the plant roots and shoots grow.

1. Study the graph.
2. What conclusions can you draw?
3. What temperature would you chose to grow these plants?

Humans and animals

14: Staying alive

Link each photograph to one of the following processes of life.

Objectives

Know that life processes common to humans and animals include nutrition (water and food), movement, growth and reproduction.

A

B

C

D

Key words reproduction nutrition growing movement

- reproduction – making new living things
- nutrition – feeding and drinking
- growing – getting larger
- movement – running, walking, sliding, flying and swimming

15: Staying alive

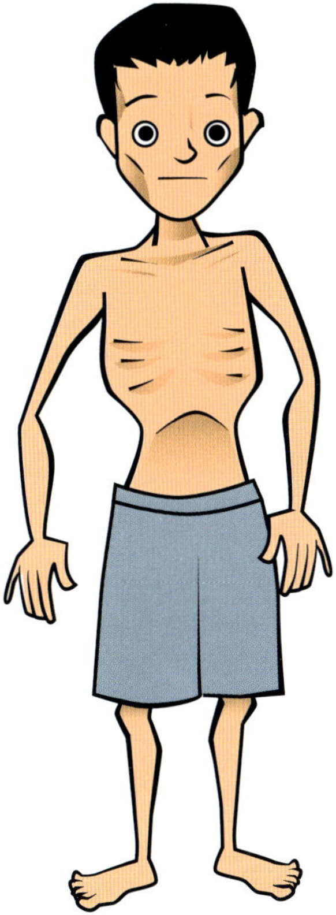

Objectives

Know that life processes common to humans and animals include nutrition (water and food), movement, growth and reproduction.

- Look at the picture.
- What do you think is happening?
- What has this person been missing?
- Write a letter to a local newspaper, including a description of the problem. List some ways in which we could help people who face this problem.

Humans and animals

16: Living or non-living?

Objectives

Describe differences between living and non-living things using knowledge of life processes.

1. Decide which of the objects above are living and which are non-living.
2. Complete a table like the one below.
3. What were the clues that you used to help you to decide?

Living	Non-living

Humans and animals

17: Movement

Objectives

Describe differences between living and non-living things using knowledge of life processes.

- Study the animals shown.
- List the different ways that the animals are moving.
- Discuss why animals need to move.
- Show a partner five different ways that you can move.

18: Taking in air

- Look at the pictures.
- Why is the person out of breath in picture B?

Objectives

Describe differences between living and non-living things using knowledge of life processes.

Investigate your breathing rate

1. Sit down quietly and count how many breaths you take in a minute. Record this in a table. This is your resting breathing rate.
2. Run on the spot for one minute, then sit down quietly and count how many breaths you take in a minute. Record this in a table. This is your breathing rate after exercise.
3. Compare your resting breathing rate with your breathing rate after exercise.
4. Explain the difference.

Talk about Investigate how we breathe.

19: Deficiency diseases

Objectives

Explore and research exercise and the adequate, varied diet needed to keep healthy.

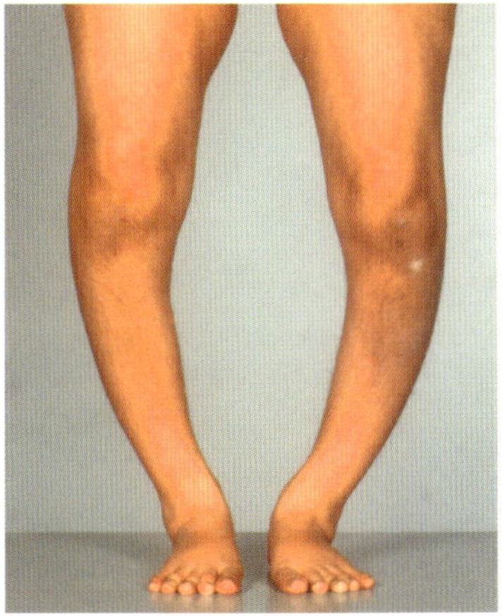

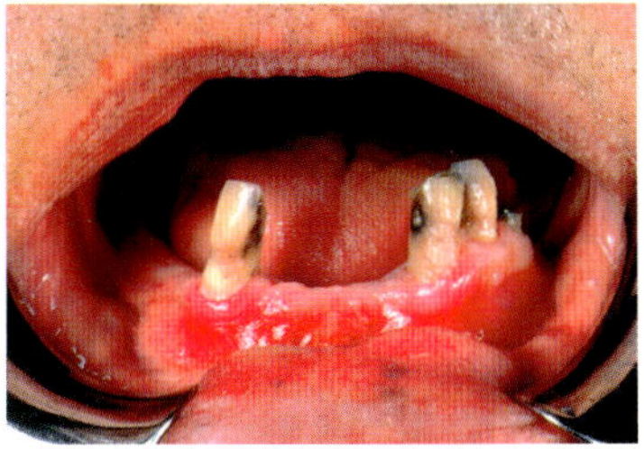

Two common diseases are shown in the pictures.

1 Use the table below to help you to identify or diagnose the diseases.

Disease	Symptoms and prevention
Scurvy	• Swollen gums that can bleed and teeth may fall out • Feeling very tired with pain in the arms and legs • Eating foods rich in vitamin C, such as fruit and vegetables, can prevent scurvy
Rickets	• People with rickets can have weak and soft bones, stunted growth, and problems with bent and damaged bones • Rickets can be prevented by eating foods with lots of vitamin D, such as fish, liver, milk and eggs

2 Write down how the two diseases can be prevented.

20: Unhealthy diets

Objectives

Explore and research exercise and the adequate, varied diet needed to keep healthy.

You are going to have a visit from a health professional. This person is going to talk to you about healthy and unhealthy diets.

1. Discuss possible questions with a partner.
2. Write down three questions you could ask the visitor about healthy eating and a healthy lifestyle.

Your teacher will help you to decide on five class questions.

1. Take some notes during the visitor's talk.
2. Write down the answers to any of the questions.
3. Work with your class to write a thank you letter to the visitor.

Talk about

Is the meal above healthy? Why?

Humans and animals

21: Food groups

Objectives

Explore and research exercise and the adequate, varied diet needed to keep healthy.

1. Study the foods shown.

2. Identify two foods that are found in each of the following food groups:

Key words proteins carbohydrates fats

3. List any protein-rich foods you have eaten today.

4. List any carbohydrate-rich foods you have eaten today.

5. List any fat-rich foods you have eaten today.

Humans and animals

22: Analysing meals

Objectives

Explore and research exercise and the adequate, varied diet needed to keep healthy.

1. Think about the food that you can chose from the school canteen.

   a. Analyse the balance of food on offer.

   b. Are the choices healthy?

2. Write a message to the person who manages the canteen.

   a. Tell them how healthy the choices are.

   b. Suggest some even healthier foods that could be available.

23: Designing healthy meals

Objectives

Explore and research exercise and the adequate, varied diet needed to keep healthy.

Different activities use up different amounts of energy. We get our energy from eating carbohydrates and fats.

1. Which of these activities uses the most energy?
2. Design a healthy meal for the person using a heavy power tool.
3. Design a healthy meal for the person sitting at the computer.
4. How should they be different?
5. Display the meals you have designed on two paper plates by drawing the foods on them. Your teacher will hang your plates to make a collage.

Humans and animals

24: Your food diary

Objectives

Know that some foods can be damaging to health, e.g. very sweet and fatty foods.

- Keep a record of all of the things you eat and drink. This is your food diary.
- Keep your diary for one week. Next to each food use a star system to show how healthy the foods are.

☆	Not very healthy – have in very small amounts or not at all
☆☆	Some health value – eat in small amounts
☆☆☆	Healthy – but do not overeat
☆☆☆☆	Very healthy – have as part of a healthy diet
☆☆☆☆☆	The healthiest foods – have as part of a healthy diet

1. Analyse your food diary at the end of the week.
2. What conclusions can you draw about how healthy your diet is?
3. What changes could you make to make it even healthier?

25: Looking after your teeth

Objectives

Know that some foods can be damaging to health, e.g. very sweet and fatty foods.

Some scientists have claimed that cola drinks will dissolve teeth.

Other people claim that fruit juices will also do this.

1. Plan your investigation. How will you make it a fair test?
2. Leave the teeth, chicken bones or egg shells in the drinks for at least a week but check them every day.
3. Record your findings
4. What are your conclusions?
5. Write a report telling people what really happens to teeth or chicken bones in different drinks.

Talk about

Do fruit and cola drinks damage teeth? (Use egg shells instead of teeth!)

26: Problems with teeth

Objectives

Know that some foods can be damaging to health, e.g. very sweet and fatty foods.

Bacteria use the sugars in food as their food. Bacteria are tiny living things.

The bacteria make acids and these can attack your teeth.

Acid foods and drinks can also damage your teeth. They cause tooth decay and gum diseases.

Your saliva helps to protect your teeth and gums. It can kill harmful bacteria and wash away acids. Brushing also helps.

1. Research how brushing your teeth can protect you from tooth decay and gum disease.
2. Design and create a poster telling people how to care for their teeth.

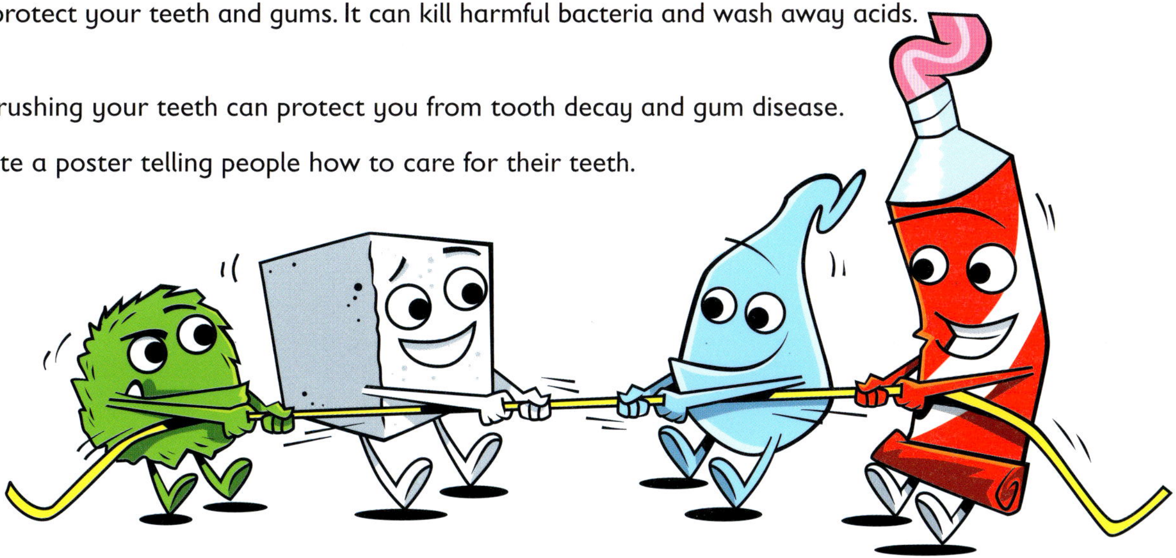

27: Obesity and being overweight

Objectives

Know that some foods can be damaging to health, e.g. very sweet and fatty foods.

Whether a person eats too much or takes too little exercise is often a lifestyle choice. Eating too much, and not exercising enough, causes people to be overweight or even obese.

1. Find out the percentage of people in your country who are overweight if the figure isn't in the chart.
2. Research how being overweight can make a person less healthy and write a short story about the need for a healthy lifestyle. Include heart disease and diabetes in your story.

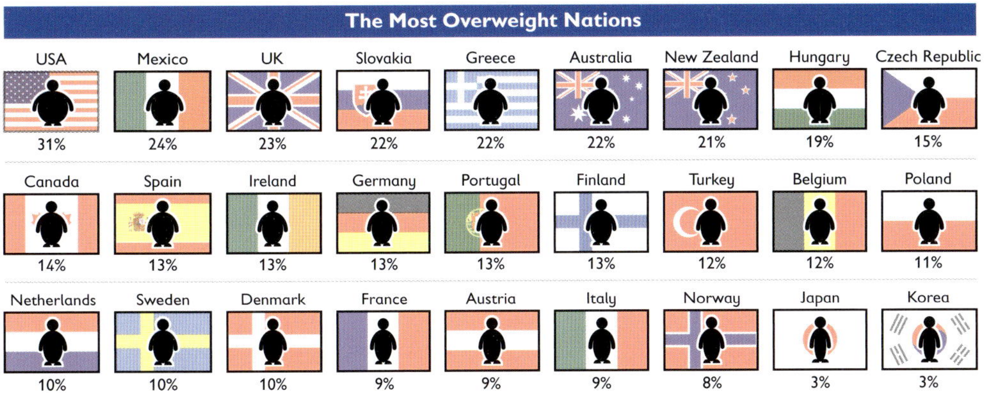

Talk about

- Work with a partner.
- Which country in the chart has the highest rate of overweight people?
- Which country in the chart has the lowest rate of overweight people?
- Discuss some reasons for the differences seen in the chart.

Humans and animals

28: Testing texture

Objectives

Explore human senses and the ways we use them to learn about our world – touch.

The human sense of touch is very delicate. You can feel very small differences in surfaces. Surfaces can be very smooth or very rough or anything in between. How a surface feels is known as its 'texture'.

1. Work with a partner. One of you wears a blindfold
2. The other person will place objects down on the table
3. The blindfolded person must gently feel the objects and describe what the texture is like.
4. Complete a table showing the texture of half of the objects.
5. Now change places and test the remaining half of the objects

Talk about

How accurate was your sense of touch?

29: Linking properties to materials

Objectives

Explore human senses and the ways we use them to learn about our world – touch.

Work with a partner.

1. Your partner will place some objects into a feely bag
2. Put your hand in the bag but do not look inside.
3. Pick up an object and describe it to your partner.
4. Predict what the object is and then remove it from the bag.
5. Complete a table showing how many objects you identified correctly.
6. Change places but use different objects.

Talk about

Which two of the following properties could you not use to identify your object?

a. texture; **b.** shininess; **c.** hardness; **d.** colour; **e.** shape

Humans and animals

30: Favourite fruit tastes

Objectives

Explore human senses and the ways we use them to learn about our world – taste.

1. Design a survey of your class to find out the two favourite fruit tastes
2. Draw a table similar to the one shown to record your results.
3. Analyse your table and calculate the two favourite fruit tastes.
4. Make a display to show your findings.

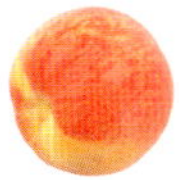	

Other	

Humans and animals

31: Tasting test

Objectives

Explore human senses and the ways we use them to learn about our world – taste.

You are going to work with a partner to carry out a taste test. Your teacher will give you some different foods or drinks.

Stay safe!

Tell your teacher if you have any food allergies or intolerances.

1. Place the foods or drinks in front of you.

Stay safe!

Make sure you have both washed your hands.

2. One person wears a blindfold.
3. The other person hands over a piece of food or drink. It must be in a container.
4. The blindfolded person must test the taste of the food or drink.
5. Keep a record of the results.
6. Take it in turn to try the test.

Talk about

- Was it easy to identify a taste without seeing the food or drink?
- Which sense organ were you using?

Humans and animals

32: Investigating taste buds

Objectives

Explore human senses and the ways we use them to learn about our world – taste.

Scientists once thought that different parts of the tongue tasted different flavours. They even produced a map of the tongue showing the areas. They now think that this isn't the case but you can test this yourself.

Your teacher will give you five containers of liquids: water, cold coffee, salty water, sugar water and lime or lemon juice. You will also need four clean straws.

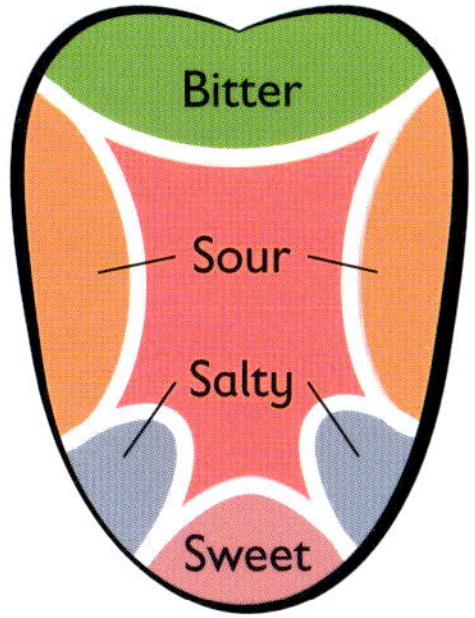

1. Look at the tongue map.
2. Place one drop of the salty liquid onto different areas of your partner's tongue. They should wash out their mouth with clean water after each drop.
3. Ask them what they taste and record the results.
4. Repeat the investigation for the other three substances.
5. Change roles and repeat the investigation.
6. What do you conclude about the tongue map?

Stay safe!

Keep all of the straws and liquids clean. Do not share straws.

33: Smell protecting us

Objectives

Explore human senses and the ways we use them to learn about our world – smell.

Our sense of smell can attract us to things. Some shops create the smell of fresh bread or coffee to attract customers. Smells can also warn us if food is not fresh. We may also detect dangerous smells such as smoke, petrol and gas.

1. Make a list of the smells you find pleasant.
2. Make a list of the smells you find unpleasant.
3. Which of these smells can protect you?
4. Write a short story about a person who detects an unpleasant smell but this turns out to protect the person and their friends.

Humans and animals

34: Inventing a scent

Objectives

Explore human senses and the ways we use them to learn about our world – smell.

You are going to make a smelly potion!

1. Collect about 30 flower petals.
2. Add a small amount of water until the petals are damp.
3. Crush the petals – this is best done with a pestle and mortar, or you could use a spoon and press the petals.
4. Pour the petals into a small dish of water and stir.
5. Strain the mixture through a sieve so you are left with only the coloured water.
6. Put this into a bottle. You have now made your perfume.
7. Think up a name for your perfume.
8. Try to make perfume from other flowers or fruits.

35: How smell works

Objectives

Explore human senses and the ways we use them to learn about our world – smell.

1. Look at the diagram showing how scent is detected by your brain.

   a. Draw a large version of it into your notebook.

   b. Add arrows to show the path of a scent moving from the air to be detected.

2. Your teacher will spray a perfume somewhere in the room.

   a. Put your hand up when you can detect it.

   b. Did everyone detect it at the same time?

   c. What does this tell you about how scents travel through the air?

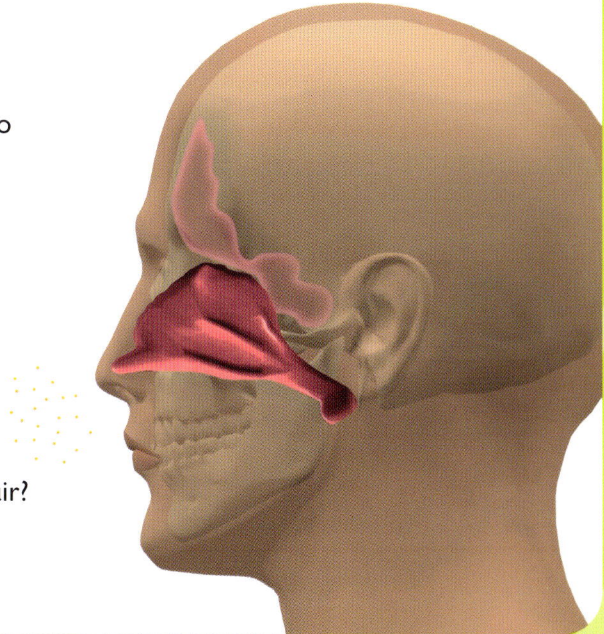

Humans and animals

36: The eye

Objectives

Explore human senses and the ways we use them to learn about our world – sight.

1. Label the parts of the eye using the key words.

Key words iris eyelid pupil sclera eyelashes eyebrow

2. Make a poster-sized version of the drawing.
3. Add a note explaining what each part of the eye does.

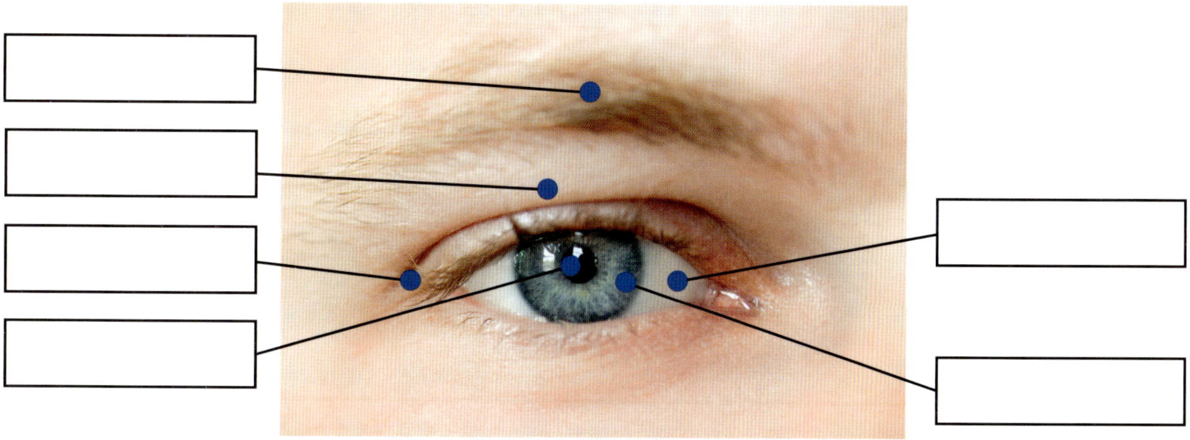

37: Tricking our sight

Objectives

Explore human senses and the ways we use them to learn about our world – sight.

Look at the pictures below. They show some optical illusions. These are pictures that trick our eyesight by showing something that looks very different from what it really is.

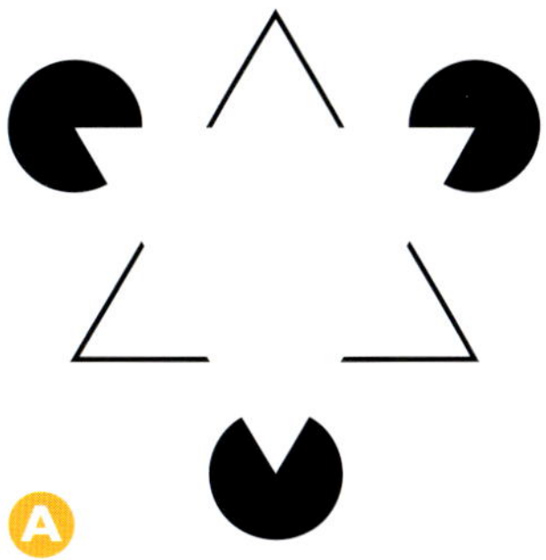

A

B

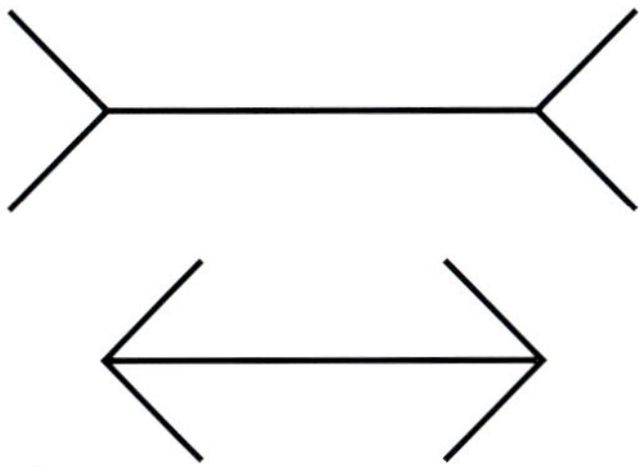

C

- How many triangles can you see in picture A?
- Is the spiral on picture B moving?
- Look at picture C. Which of the two central lines is longer?

Humans and animals

38: Listening to nature

Objectives

Explore human senses and the ways we use them to learn about our world – hearing.

1. Go outside to carry out a sound survey.
   - **a.** Stand quietly for five minutes.
   - **b.** Write down any sounds that you hear.
   - **c.** Record them in a table similar to the one below.

Sound	How often did I hear it?	Natural or man-made?

2. When you go back to your classroom, study your table and produce a graph of your results.
   - **a.** Which sound was the most common?
   - **b.** Which sounds did you expect to hear but didn't?
   - **c.** Which sound was the most surprising?

Humans and animals

39: Why do we have two ears?

Objectives

Explore human senses and the ways we use them to learn about our world – hearing.

1. Work with a small group.
2. Form a circle.
3. One person sits in the middle of the circle.
4. They cup their ears but close their eyes.
5. The people in a circle take it in turns to clap.
6. The person in the middle points to where they think the sound comes from.
7. Take turns so that everyone can be in the middle.

Talk about

- If the ears are cupped the other way, is the sound detected in the same way?
- If the left ear is covered, is the sound detected in the same way?
- If the right ear is covered, is the sound detected in the same way?

Humans and animals

40: Grouping living things

Objectives

Sort living things into groups, using simple features, and describe rationale for groupings.

1. Name as many of the animals shown as you can.
2. Make a list and organise the animals into different groups. Use the characteristics you can observe to help you do this.
3. How many groups did you form?
4. Write down what all of the living things have in common.

Talk about

Compare your groups with the groups made by other people. Did you all agree?

Chemistry

Material properties

1: Looking at properties of materials

Objectives

Know that every material has specific properties, e.g. hard, soft, shiny.

1. Make a list of all the properties that you can name.
2. Walk around your classroom looking for materials.
3. Test each material to find out what the properties are.
4. Record the material, where you found it and the properties that the material has.

Talk about

Talk to your partner about different properties of materials.

Material properties

2: Materials detective

Objectives

Know that every material has specific properties, e.g. hard, soft, shiny.

You are going to match the material to the description. Work in pairs. One person will read out a description and the other has to identify the material being described.

1. This material can be seen through and is very shiny and hard.
2. This material can be stretched and bent easily.
3. This material is very strong, hard and shiny. It can be formed into different shapes and objects.
4. This material is white in colour and leaves a mark when scratched against dark surfaces.

Key words rubber glass chalk metal

Material properties

3: Sorting materials

Objectives

Sort materials according to their properties.

1. Work with a partner to look at the pictures.
2. Can you name any of the objects?
3. What material is each of the objects made from?
4. What are the properties of the materials being used?
5. Record your observations.

Talk about Talk about why that material was chosen for the object.

Material properties

4: Materials display

Objectives

Sort materials according to their properties.

You are going to find a picture of a material or a sample of a material that has one of the following properties:

Key words soft hard shiny waterproof rough smooth

1. Copy the name of each property onto a label or sticky note. These will be the labels for sorting.
2. Find materials and pictures of materials around the room and place them under the correct property heading.
3. Look for pictures in magazines or on the internet and put them under the correct heading.

Material properties

5: Magnetic materials

Objectives

Explore how some materials are magnetic but many are not.

1. Look around the room and find an object that you think will be attracted to a magnet. We say such objects are 'magnetic'.
2. Write down the names of the magnetic objects.
3. Then find an object that you predict will not be attracted to a magnet. We say these are 'not magnetic'.
4. Your teacher will give you a magnet to test the objects.
5. Was your prediction correct?
6. Now you have practised predicting and testing magnetic materials, find more objects. Try to find six objects that you predict will be attracted to the magnet and six that will not.
7. Test your predictions and record your observations.

Material properties

6: Investigating magnetic materials

Objectives

Explore how some materials are magnetic but many are not.

You are going to work as part of a team for this card activity. Your teacher will give you a secret package.

1. You and your team have to plan an investigation to find out if the contents of the package are magnetic.
2. You are not allowed to open the package.
3. Plan an investigation to test the secret package.
4. Decide as a group if you predict that the contents of the package will be magnetic or non-magnetic.

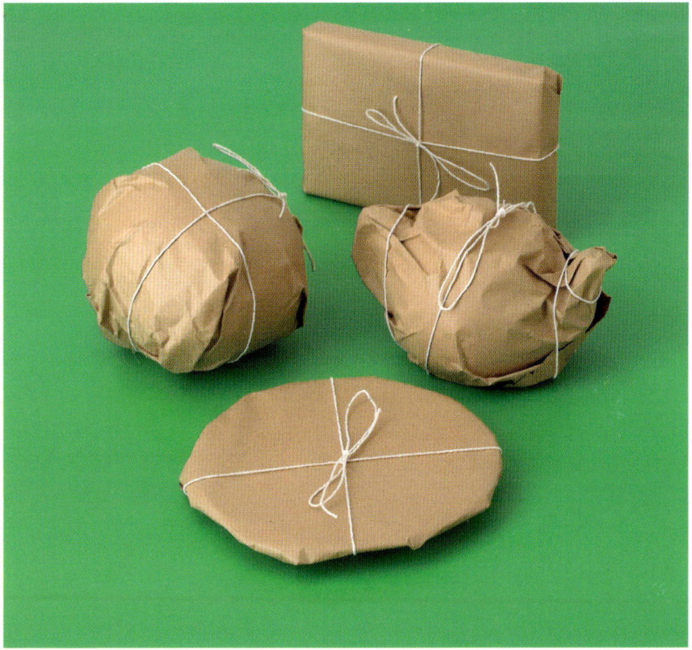

Material properties

7: Being an inventor

Objectives

Discuss why materials are chosen for specific purposes on the basis of their properties.

Look at the picture with a partner. The student shows many uses of different materials.

1. List the objects that you can see.
2. Decide the material that each of the objects is made from.
3. Think about other materials that each object could be made from.
4. Would this improve the object or not?
5. Explain your answer.

Material properties

8: Which material is the most absorbent?

Objectives

Discuss why materials are chosen for specific purposes on the basis of their properties.

- Look at the picture. What is the person in the picture doing?
- What are they using? Have you ever done this?

You are going to work in a team to find out which materials clean up spills the best. Your teacher will give you four different materials.

1. Make sure that each material is the same size.
2. Measure 300cm^3 of water using a measuring jug.
3. Fold the first material you are going to test into four.
4. Place the folded paper into the water and leave it for 2 minutes.
5. Remove the paper but let it drip over the jug for a minute.
6. Measure the water left in the jug.
7. The more absorbent material will soak up more water and leave less in the jug than a less absorbent material.
8. Record your results and compare them.
9. Which material was the most absorbent?

Material properties

9: Choosing materials for a purpose

Objectives

Discuss why materials are chosen for specific purposes on the basis of their properties.

Which is the best floor covering for a certain location?

Some shiny and smooth surfaces can be very dangerous when they are wet.

You are going to investigate surfaces around the school. Your teacher will give you a forcemeter and a shoe.

1. Attach the forcemeter to the shoe and pull it until the shoe moves across the surface.
2. Record the measurement on the forcemeter.
3. Repeat this on four more surfaces around the school.
4. Which surface was the most slippery?
5. Which was the least?

Talk about

Talk to your partner about the picture. What would happen if you ran on this surface?

Material properties

10: Choosing the best material

Objectives

Discuss why materials are chosen for specific purposes on the basis of their properties.

1. Look at the pictures and think about when you would wear them.
   - **a.** What do the materials need to do?
   - **b.** Will they keep you warm or cool?
   - **c.** How would you put them on?
2. Your teacher will give you some samples of materials.
   - **a.** Choose the one that would be best for each of the items of clothing.
   - **b.** Explain why you have chosen each material.
   - **c.** Present your ideas to the class.
   - **d.** Compare your ideas with others.

Physics

Forces and motion

1: Pushes and pulls

Objectives

Know that pushes and pulls are examples of forces and that they can be measured with forcemeters.

Look at the picture and try to find where forces are being used.

The next time you are playing or when you are doing things today, think about whether you are using pushes or pulls.

Talk about

- Talk to your partner about where you can see a push force or a pull force.
- Are there any activities where you could use both a push or pull force?

Forces and motion

2: Using a forcemeter

Objectives

Know that pushes and pulls are examples of forces and that they can be measured with forcemeters.

Work in a small group or team to investigate how the forcemeter works.

- Look at the scale on the forcemeter.
- What units are used to measure force? (Remember that weight is a force and so it is not measured in grams or kilograms.)
- Attach a carrier bag or container to the hook.
- You can then measure different objects using the forcemeter.

Hint

Make sure that the bag is strong enough to hold the object without breaking.

Forces and motion

3: Comparing grams to newtons

Objectives

Know that pushes and pulls are examples of forces and that they can be measured with forcemeters.

Look at the picture of the supermarket scales. You might have used scales like this or digital ones to measure food.

Hint

Remember that weight is a force and should be measured in newtons.

1. Use a set of scales to measure five different objects. Record the measurements.
2. Now use a forcemeter and record these measurements.
3. Are the measurements the same?
4. Can you see a pattern?

Talk about

- What units of measurement do the scales use?
- Is this the correct unit?

Forces and motion

4: Using forces

Objectives

Explore how forces can make objects start or stop moving.

Look at the picture of the children playing with the cars. Your teacher will give you some toy cars. Move the cars back and forth and then answer the questions.

1. How can you make the cars move forwards?
2. How can you make the cars move backwards?
3. How can you make the cars move slower?
4. How can you make the cars move faster?
5. Can you stop the cars moving?

Forces and motion

5: Using forces to stop a moving ball

Objectives

Explore how forces can make objects start or stop moving.

You are going to work with a partner to investigate how to make a ball roll and then how to stop it using just one other ball.

1. Sit on the floor like the people in the picture.
2. One person will make a ball roll in a straight line across the floor.
3. The other person has to try to stop this first ball from moving in a straight line by using another ball.
4. Next, try to stop the ball or speed it up, using only the second ball.
5. What forces did you use?

6: Making shapes with paper

Objectives

Explore how forces can change the shape of objects.

Your teacher will give you a sheet of paper.

1. Follow the instructions to try to make a paper hat. You could work with a partner to help each other.
2. Try to design and make different objects from paper. You could try an aeroplane or a boat, for example.
3. Identify the pushes and pulls that you use to make the hat.

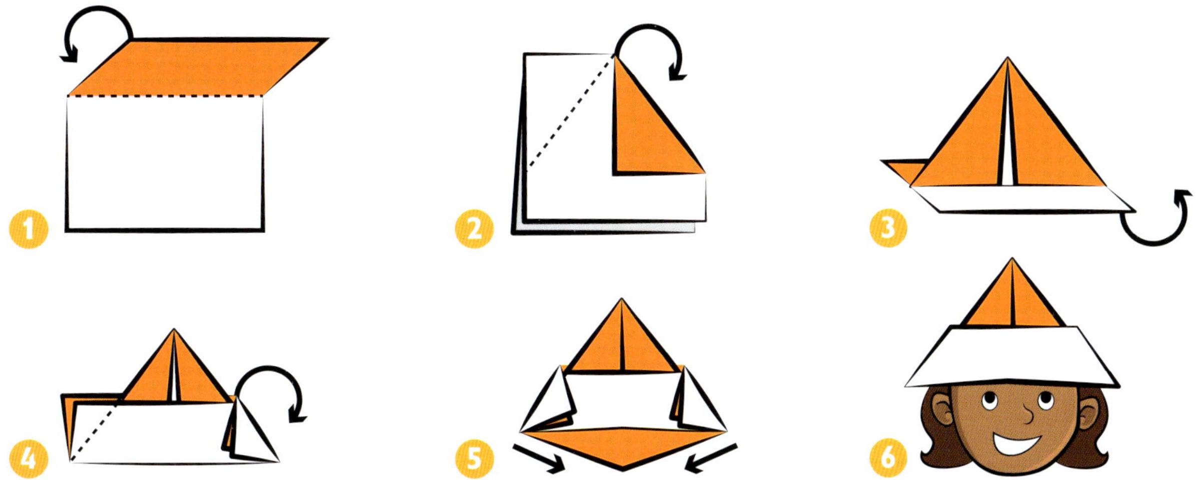

Forces and motion

7: Changing the shape of modelling clay

Objectives

Explore how forces can change the shape of objects.

You will work in a group for this activity.

Your teacher will give you a modelling material.

1. Explore how you can change the shape of it.
2. Discuss in your team what force is being used and how this changes the shape of the material.
3. Design a model that you can make using forces to change the shape of the material.
4. Make the model and put it on display in the science corner or classroom.
5. Compare your model to the others.

Talk about

Look at the picture. Discuss how the child is changing the shape of the modelling material. What actions is she taking?

8: Pushes and pulls survey

Objectives

Explore how forces can change the shape of objects

Look at the picture.

You are going to work in a research team to find objects that have changed shape using pushes and pulls.

1. You could take pictures of the objects you find or make drawings of them.
2. Explain to your team how pushes and pulls might have been used to change the shape.

Talk about

- What shape is the metal being made into?
- How is the person making the flat metal change shape?

Forces and motion

9: Friction is a force

Objectives

Explore how forces, including friction, can make objects move faster or slower or change direction.

1. What is the person doing?
2. Why are they doing this?
3. Have you ever done this before?
4. Rub your hands together. Describe to your partner how your hands feel.

This happens because of a force called 'friction'. When surfaces rub together, friction occurs. This can be very useful when using brakes or to stop your boots slipping on ice.

Talk about Talk to your partner about the picture.

Forces and motion

10: Which trainer has the best grip?

Objectives

Explore how forces, including friction, can make objects move faster or slower or change direction.

You are going to work as part of a team to investigate which shoes have the best grip. Your teacher will give you a piece of wood or a tile to make a ramp and a variety of shoes and trainers.

1. Plan an investigation to find out which shoe will cause the most friction with the surface of the ramp. (The one with the most friction will have the most grip and move the least on the ramp.)
2. Look at the soles of the shoes and trainers and predict which one will have the best grip.
3. Design a method to test your prediction.
4. Draw a suitable table to record your observations.
5. Carry out the investigation.
6. Look at your results. Was your prediction correct?